Handmade Celtic Cards

Paula Pascual

SEARCH PRESS

First published in Great Britain 2008

Search Press Limited,
Wellwood, North Farm Road,
Tunbridge Wells, Kent TN2 3DR

ISBN: 978-1-84448-260-3

The Publishers and author can accept no responsibility for any consequences arising from the information, advice or instructions given in this publication.

Readers are permitted to reproduce any of the items in this book for their personal use, or for the purposes of selling for charity, free of charge and without the prior permission of the Publishers. Any use of the items for commercial purposes is not permitted without the prior permission of the Publishers.

Suppliers

For details of suppliers, please visit the Search Press website: www.searchpress.com

Although every attempt has been made to ensure that all the materials and equipment used in this book are currently available, the Publishers cannot guarantee that this will always be the case. If you have difficulty in obtaining any of the items mentioned, then suitable alternatives should be used instead.

Publishers' note

All the step-by-step photographs in this book feature the author, Paula Pascual, demonstrating how to make Celtic greetings cards. No models have been used.

Printed in Malaysia.

Dedication

To my sister Ananda, who has always truly inspired me to be a better person and therefore a better crafter.

Acknowledgements

Thank you to all the people involved in making this book: Roz Dace and Caroline de la Bédoyère for choosing me to write it; Katie Sparkes for being a wonderful editor; and the photographers, Debbie Patterson and Gavin Sawyer.

Thank you to all the suppliers of gorgeous Celtic craft materials: Rebekah of Heritage Rubber Stamps for supplying me with the best images; Ada and Andrew of Kars for always delivering what I required; Judith of Woodware for the stencils and paste; Jayne of Personal Impressions for the pens and stamps; Ruth of Stix 2 for the sticky stuff and to Sue at Craftwork Cards for the superior quality card.

I wish to thank also my crafter friends who have taught me so much: Dawn Bibby, Leonie Pujol, Jane Gill, Caroline Counsel, Kim Reygate, Sarah McGrath and, especially, Julie Hickey who has done so much for me that were I to list it all it would probably fill the pages of this book.

Thank you to my parents, Angel and Elvira, and also my Uncle Vicente, who have all made this book possible, by teaching and inspiring me with their art since I was a little girl.

And, finally, I would like to thank Omar for being so understanding of all my craft passions and obsessions.

Cover
Celtic Circle, page 25.

Title page
Variation on the Spiral of Light project (see page 47).

Contents

Projects

Introduction

I couldn't say when it all started, but my fascination with all things Celtic – whether it be design, symbolism, music, history or art – goes back a long way, to when I was a child on the Spanish island of Mallorca. The intrinsic beauty of the Celts is eternal, and goes beyond the barriers of time. Being able to combine it with my biggest craft passion, papercrafting, is a fantastic opportunity for me.

When I am teaching or demonstrating cardmaking, people often ask me to share my ideas on how to make cards for the men in their life. I tried to keep this in mind when I was designing the cards for this book, and therefore included a number of cards with a more masculine appeal. I also wanted to show that Celtic designs can work well on cards for many special celebrations, for example Christmas and for welcoming a new baby.

In the project on page 43 I have provided a template from the book *Celtic Designs* by Courtney Davis, published in the *Design Source Book* series by Search Press/Gill & Macmillan. This book, together with *Celtic Knotwork Designs* by Elaine Hill, *Celtic Borders and Motifs* by Lesley Davis and *The Complete Book of Celtic Designs*, all published by Search Press/Gill & Macmillan, represent a rich source of designs, patterns and inspiration.

The best thing I can say to you is this: have fun experimenting with all the techniques and ideas in this book, and I hope they will inspire you to create beautiful Celtic designs of your own.

A selection of greetings cards that you can make using the techniques described in this book.

Materials and equipment

When it comes to materials, the rule should always be: buy the best that you can afford. Be careful, though, as the highest-priced products are not necessarily the best quality. You do not need to purchase everything at once; you can start with a few essentials and build up your own collection over time.

Papers and card

It is essential, when cardmaking, to have a proper assortment of coloured and pearlescent card. Start with the basic colours – white and cream, for example – and a few of your favourites, then build up a small collection from there. I prefer to buy single sheets of card and then cut and score them to my desired shape and size, though ready-made card blanks are available from craft suppliers. The best weight to use for greetings cards is between 240 and 280gsm.

A collection of coloured papers, like card, can be built up over time, beginning with just a few basic colours. Patterned papers can be bought as individual sheets or in themed books or packs. Metallic papers are a perfect way of adding a metal effect without the weight or cost of metallic card or metal sheet, though the latter can be embossed to create a beautiful three-dimensional design which has a shine and lustre that cannot be achieved with metallic paper or card.

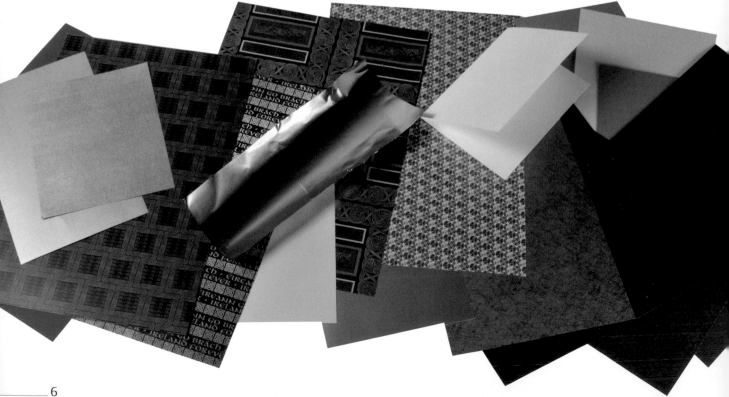

Basic equipment

The photograph below shows all the basic equipment you will need to get started. It includes: a **cutting mat** to protect your table surface when cutting and inking; a **metal ruler** for measuring and marking lines, and for cutting along; a **pencil** to mark paper or card for scoring and cutting (a soft pencil will be easier to erase); an **eraser** to remove the pencil marks; **tweezers** for holding and positioning delicate items; **scissors** and a **craft knife** for cutting (paper and card make them blunt over time so make sure you buy a new pair of scissors regularly, and replace the blade in the craft knife for more precise work); **miniature scissors** for cutting round intricate details; a **bone folder**, originally a bookbinder's tool – use this to score and define the folds in your card (this will become one of the most used tools in your set); a **paper trimmer** to cut paper and card quickly and accurately (buy which ever model works best for you); **PVA glue**, and either **double-sided adhesive tape** or an **adhesive roller** for attaching papers and embellishments to your card; **3D adhesive foam pads** for achieving a three-dimensional, decoupage look; **glue pens** for attaching tiny items such as gemstones or to apply a quick coat of glitter; **eye-shadow applicators** for applying decorative chalk and **cotton buds** for dabbing on inks; **low-tack tape**, which is indispensable for positioning or holding items in place temporarily; **artists' sealant spray** or cheap **hairspray** (the cheaper the hairspray the better, as it contains less oil than more expensive varieties and therefore will do less damage to your paper or card); a **spatula** for spreading out embossing paste evenly; **round-ended** and **pointed embossing tools** for stencil embossing (they can also be used instead of a bone folder for scoring card); and a **foam mat** to put underneath metal sheet while embossing. A **circle cutting system**, though not essential, is excellent for cutting different-sized circles accurately, and similarly a **stamp positioner** is useful for ensuring you always stamp in the right place.

Materials for creating patterns

There are many ways of transferring a Celtic pattern or design to your card. Rubber stamps are the easiest and quickest way. Polymer stamps are also available, which are transparent and therefore easier to position. An image stamped on to transparency paper can be coloured with alcohol inks for a jewel-like finish.

Brass stencils, used in conjunction with embossing tools and embossing paste, allow you to create elegant motifs with a subtle three-dimensional effect on metal sheet.

Craft stickers are available in many different designs, and are an inexpensive and easy way to add a metallic image to your card.

Materials for adding colour

All crafters should have a permanent black ink pad in their basic kit for stamping images on to card. A watermark ink pad is also extremely useful. It can be used not only to create a subtle, translucent image, but also as an embossing ink pad. You can emboss the image by sprinkling it with embossing powder (which adheres to the outline), tipping off the excess and then heating to produce a raised, metallic design.

Embossing paste, used in conjunction with a brass stencil, is another, simple, way of creating a raised image. It is also useful for strengthening an image embossed on to metal sheet – spreading it over the back of the design will prevent the surface indentations from being compressed.

Alcohol inks are a fantastic medium to use on non-porous surfaces such as metal and plastic. The intense jewel-like colours mix freely on the surface producing spectacular effects. Alcohol blending solution is used in conjunction with the inks to lighten the colours where necessary, or to remove colour where it is not needed.

Coloured chalks and pearlescent pigment powders can be used to add more subtle hints of colour to your designs. Apply them using a soft paintbrush. Chalks produce a powdery, soft finish whereas pearlescent pigment powders add a shimmering touch; mix the latter with gum arabic to create pearlescent watercolour paints that can be applied with a water brush. The handle of the water brush consists of a reservoir of water which keeps the end of the brush continually supplied with water. It is therefore ideal for blending and applying colour without the need for a pot of water.

A touch of clear glitter, applied sparingly, is always a great addition to your cards. For a really professional finish, apply gold leaf to small areas of your design. It will make your card glimmer beautifully when it catches the light. Imitation gold leaf looks almost as good as the real thing but at a fraction of the cost.

Felt-tip pens are perfect for adding colour to the tiniest of details. Soufflé pens are a more recent addition to the crafter's kit. It is a type of gel pen that work well on non-porous surfaces. They dry to a beautifully matt, opaque finish and are available in a range of pastel shades.

Making a card

Although ready-made card blanks are widely available, making your own cards gives you a limitless choice of sizes and shapes, and can be far more satisfying. Make sure, though, that ready-made envelopes are available that fit your chosen size of card.

Cutting and scoring a card are two simple but important techniques to master so that you can make your own blank cards out of any flat card available.

YOU WILL NEED

One sheet of A4 card

Retractable pencil or sharp pencil

Metal ruler

Cutting mat

Bone folder

Paper trimmer

Eraser

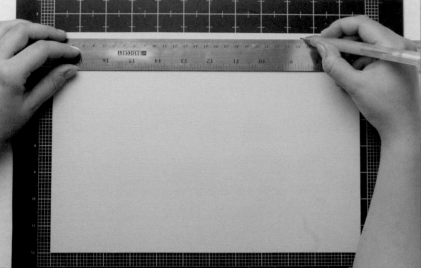

1 Align the sheet of card with the grid on the cutting mat, with the longer edges positioned widthways. Measure a distance twice the width of the greetings card along the top edge of the card (in this case 24cm, or 9½in). Mark the distance with a pencil.

2 Use a paper trimmer to cut off the excess card.

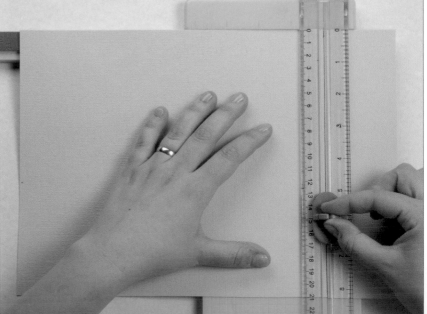

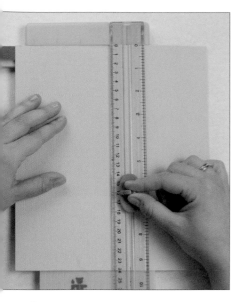

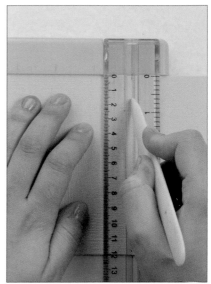

3 Measure 12cm (4¾in) along the shorter edge of the card and trim to size in the same way.

4 Find the centre of the card (where the fold will be) and mark it at the top and the bottom.

5 Place the card under the paper trimmer and score down the centre line using the bone folder.

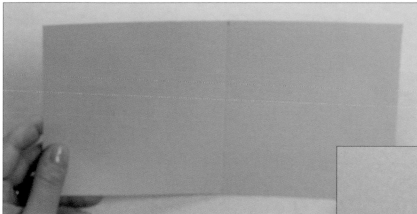

6 Remove the card and fold it in half, ensuring the indentation is on the inside.

7 Erase the pencil marks and run the bone folder firmly along the fold.

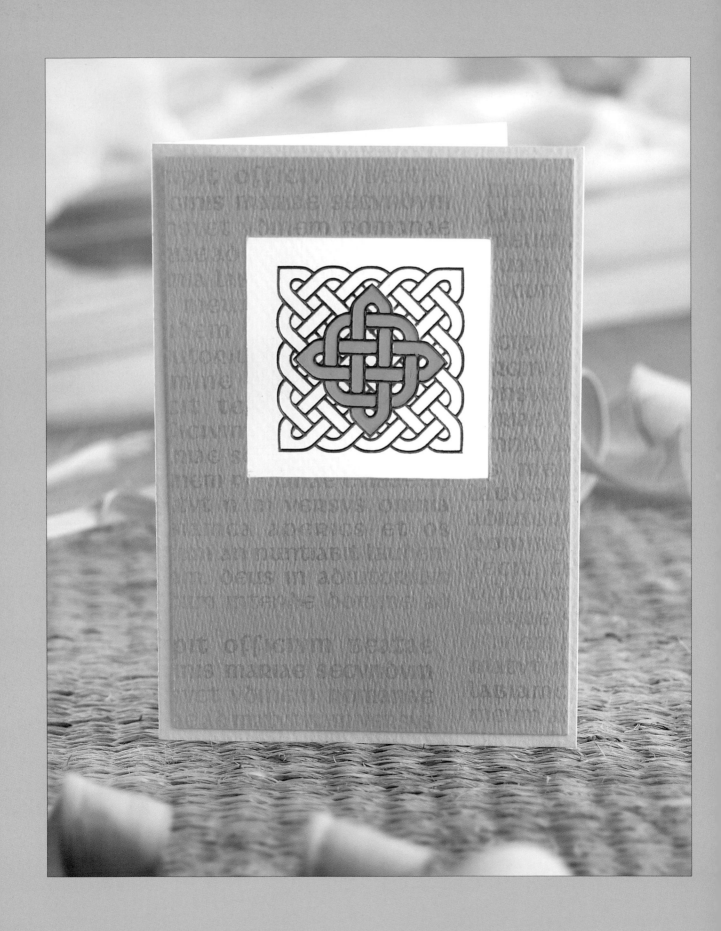

Golden Knotwork

Craft stickers are one of the best value items in paper crafting. Here you will use them to create a subtle Celtic design. The way the image appears to 'float' on the acetate is quite spectacular. I have used a soufflé pen to colour the image – this dries to a beautiful matt finish and is wonderfully easy to use.

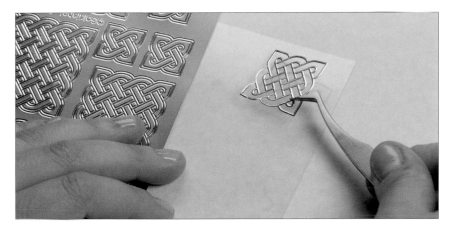

1 Using a pair of angled tweezers, remove a craft sticker that is approximately 2.5cm (1in) square from the sheet and lay it on the acetate.

YOU WILL NEED

White A6 card blank, approx. 10 x 14.5cm (4 x 5¾in)

One sheet of square Celtic craft stickers in gold, e.g. Gold Label, 547

One sheet of acetate

One sheet of A4 pale blue card

One sheet of scrap paper

Small piece of red card, at least 6cm (2¼in) square

Angled tweezers

Light blue soufflé pen

Large background script rubber stamp, e.g. Heritage Rubber Stamp Co., Celt6XLS1

Watermark ink pad

Large and a medium-sized paintbrush

Light blue pearlescent pigment powder

Cheap hairspray or fixative

Adhesive roller or double-sided tape

Cutting mat

Craft knife

Pair of small, sharp scissors

Small 3D foam pads

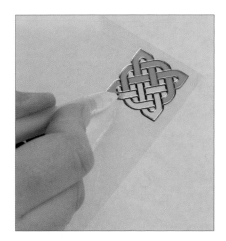

2 Colour in the design using a light blue soufflé pen. Allow it to dry completely. This usually takes two to three hours.

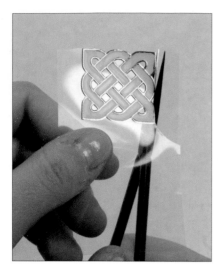

3 Trim closely around the design using a pair of small, sharp scissors. Put this to one side.

4 Cut a piece of pale blue card approximately 0.5cm (¼in) smaller all round than the front of the card blank.

5 Ink the rubber stamp using a watermark ink pad. Make sure the whole surface of the stamp is covered evenly.

6 Stamp the image on to the blue card. Work on a sheet of scrap paper, and begin by positioning the stamp slightly off the top and left-hand edges of the card. Reposition the stamp two or three times to ensure the whole surface of the card is covered.

7 Using a dry paintbrush, dab light blue pearlescent pigment powder evenly over the design.

8 Remove the excess powder using a large, dry brush. Spray the card with either cheap hairspray or fixative to seal the powder.

9 Cut a small piece of red card 6cm (2¼in) square. Using an adhesive roller or double-sided tape, attach the red square to the blue stamped card where you wish to position the aperture.

10 Working on a cutting mat, cut around the red square using a craft knife.

11 Lay the blue card on the front of the card blank, place the red square in the aperture and remove the blue card, leaving the red card in place.

12 Open out the card blank, holding the red card in position, and cut around the red square to create the aperture.

13 Lift out the piece of red card.

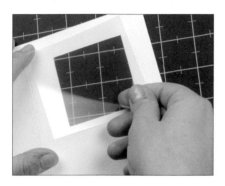

14 Cut a piece of acetate slightly larger than the aperture. Attach it to the front of the card blank over the aperture using the adhesive roller or double-sided tape.

15 Attach the stamped blue card to the front of the card blank.

16 Remove a craft sticker approximately 4.5cm (1¾in) square from the sheet and position it centrally on the acetate covering the aperture.

17 Take the blue Celtic design you made earlier and cover the back of it with small 3D foam pads.

18 Position the blue Celtic design in a diamond shape in the centre of the aperture to complete the card.

The subtle pearlescent pink card below right uses two different craft stickers from the same set as used in the project. The main motif is over an acetate window, but instead of using soufflé pens to colour it I used glaze pens to give a stained glass effect.

The copper and black card is a simpler version of the main card, and is perfect to give to a man on any occasion. If you do not have, or do not want to make, an aperture, this is an excellent alternative.

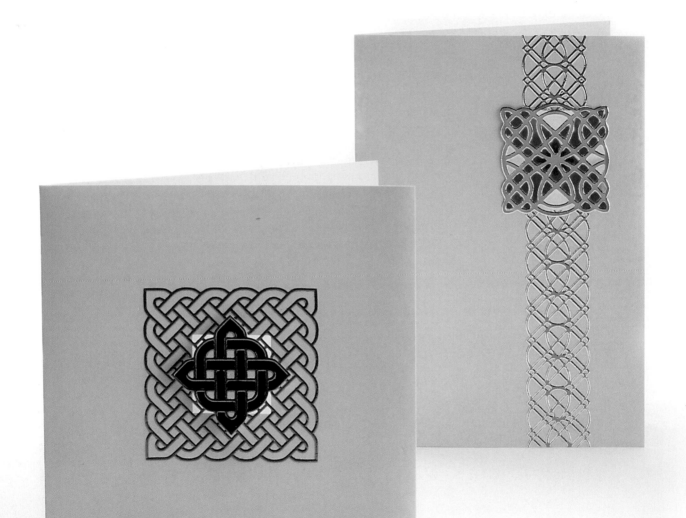

Match the colour of the soufflé pen with the background to give unity to a card, as shown in the light green and black card below left. Attach some ribbon to the back of the motif to add texture and a vertical element.

The card shown below right takes this project another step further. Here I used a trifold card with a double aperture. The acetate and craft sticker are attached to the aperture that is on the right-hand flap of the card so that the motif is visible through the aperture on the left-hand flap.

Silver Gate

This gatefold card involves three different techniques for achieving some wonderful effects: stencilling with brass stencils, embossing and chalking. I have used two embossing methods: the first uses embossing tools to create a raised image, and the second uses embossing paste, which is specially designed to be used with brass stencils and dries to a metallic finish.

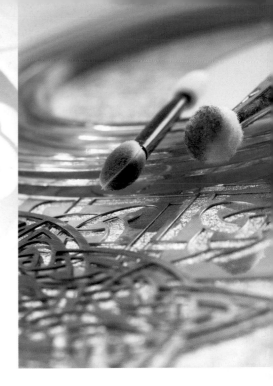

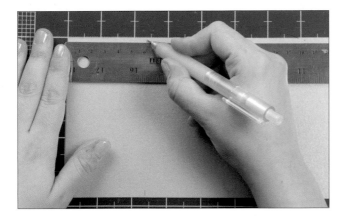

1 To make a gatefold card, first place the silver card on a cutting mat and align it with the grid so that the longer edges run widthways. Measure 6cm (2¼in) in from each edge along the top and the bottom, and mark with a pencil.

2 Fold in each side and strengthen the folds using a bone folder, following the method on page 11.

YOU WILL NEED

One sheet of silver card, 24 x 12cm (9½ x 4¾in)

Small piece of dark blue card, at least 10cm (4in) square

Small piece of silver card, at least 10cm (4in) square

Cutting mat

Retractable pencil or sharp pencil

Metal ruler

Circular Celtic brass stencil, e.g. Dreamweaver, LL380

Rectangular Celtic brass stencil, e.g. Marianne Designs, CT6004

Low-tack tape

Silver embossing paste

Spatula

Circle cutting system

Double-sided adhesive tape

Bone folder

Greaseproof paper

Light blue chalk

Small foam eye-shadow applicator

Eraser

Embossing tool

3 Attach the circular brass stencil to the piece of blue card using four strips of low-tack tape, one along each edge of the stencil.

4 Spread silver embossing paste over the back of the design using a spatula. Smooth it over so that the paste fills the design.

5 Carefully remove three of the four low-tack tape strips.

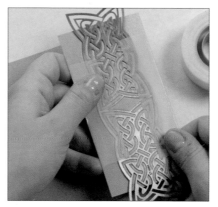

7 Meanwhile, attach the rectangular brass stencil to the front of the right-hand flap of the card blank using low-tack tape.

6 Gently lift up the stencil, leaving it secured on one side, revealing the design underneath. Remove the stencil completely, clean it, and allow the paste to dry.

8 Open up the card and rub firmly over the back of the stencil using the end of a bone folder wrapped in greaseproof paper. The indented design will gradually appear.

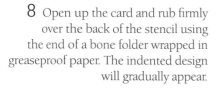

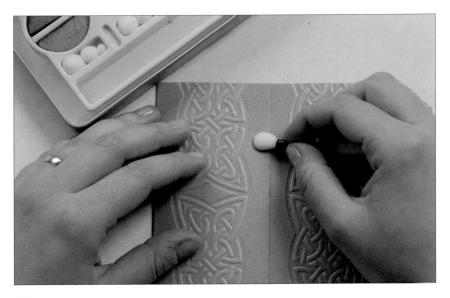

9 Using an embossing tool, press firmly over the indentations to deepen them and strengthen the design. Repeat on the left-hand flap of the card.

10 Use blue chalk applied with a small foam eye-shadow applicator to the front of the card, down the sides of the design.

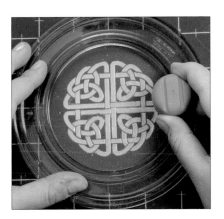

11 Remove excess chalk with an eraser for a more subtle finish.

12 Working on a cutting mat, use a circle cutting system to cut around the design. Leave a wide blue border.

13 Cut out a silver circle slightly larger than the blue. Attach the blue circle to the silver using double-sided tape.

14 Attach the motif to the left-hand flap on the front of the card.

For the card below I used a stencil (Marianne Design, CT6004) as a simple embossed background and left it plain. On a red card I used white embossing paste over a circular brass stencil (Dreamweaver, LL326 'Hearts Knot'). Once the paste is dry, you can colour it with any coloured chalks. Alternatively, you can use silver embossing paste.

To achieve the matt black finish on this card I have used black embossing paste with a circular brass stencil (Dreamweaver, LL520 'Love Knot'), which works well in combination with the rubber-stamped circular border used in the next project (Heritage Rubber Stamp Co., Celt6XLS3).

You can also use brass stencils as a cutting guide to create apertures, as I have done here with this Marianne Design, CT6002. First I embossed the image on to white paper, then I coloured it with green chalks and finally I cut out the petal-shaped details with a craft knife. To make the most of the aperture I used thick (220gsm) vellum for the green card blank and red 100gsm vellum on top, which allows the light to show through.

This cross motif is perfect for an Easter, christening or sympathy card. Here I have embossed the card using a brass stencil (Dreamweaver, LG647 'Celtic Cross') and coloured it with chalks, for which it is best to use non-glossy card. I then trimmed away the centre aperture and the edges so that I could raise the image with 3D foam pads.

Celtic Circle

This design uses different rubber stamps to create a beautiful aperture card. I have shown you how to cut out the circular aperture yourself using a circle cutting system, but ready-made circular aperture cards are available. Use good quality felt-tip pens to colour the image, and gold embossing powders to create the raised gold patterns. You will find a stamp positioner extremely useful for this project, to position the gold border accurately.

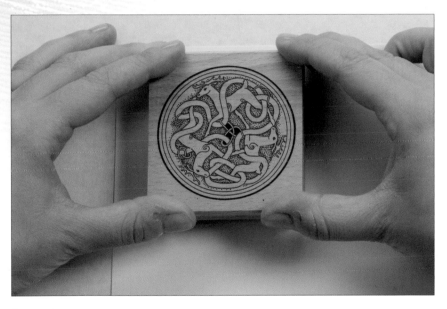

1 Apply embossing ink to the rubber stamp, and stamp the image on to the white card.

YOU WILL NEED

One sheet of A4 white card

Red card blank, 13.5cm (5¼in) square

Circular Celtic rubber stamp with animal design, e.g. Heritage Rubber Stamp Co., Celt4XLS14

Circular Celtic border rubber stamp, e.g. Heritage Rubber Stamp Co., Celt6XLS3

Small Celtic spiral rubber stamp, e.g. Heritage Rubber Stamp Co., CeltLS6

Watermark ink pad

Black ink pad

Gold embossing powder

Heat gun

Red, blue and green fine fibre-tip pens

Stamp positioner

Circle cutting system

Cutting mat

Double-sided adhesive tape

2 Cover the image in gold embossing powder.

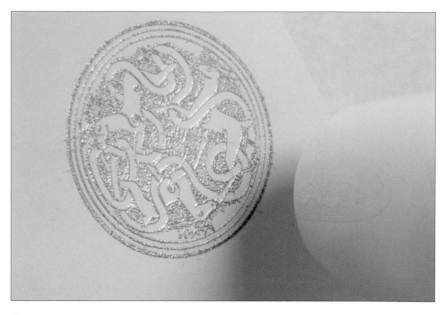

3 Tip the excess powder back into the pot. Use a heat gun to heat the image. Hold the gun approximately 10cm (4in) from the surface and stop heating as soon as the embossing powder melts and becomes shiny.

4 Colour in the three animals and the border using the red, blue and green felt-tip pens. Put this to one side and allow to dry.

5 Use the stamp positioner to position the circular border on the card accurately. First, align the acrylic sheet supplied with the stamp positioner with the L-shape. Then apply the black ink pad to the rubber stamp and transfer the image to the acrylic sheet, positioning the wooden block so that it, too, is aligned with the L-shape.

6 Place the inked acrylic sheet on top of the red card. Position the circular design accurately by eye.

7 Align the L-shape with the acrylic sheet as before, holding the acrylic sheet in position on the card.

8 Holding the L-shape in place, remove the acrylic sheet.

9 Ink the circular border stamp with embossing ink and apply the image to the card, aligning the wooden block with the L-shape as before.

10 Emboss the image using gold embossing powder (see steps 2 and 3).

11 Open out the card and, working on a cutting mat, use the circle cutting system to cut out an aperture within the border, just slightly larger than the circular image you made earlier.

12 Stamp the small spiral design randomly over the front of the card using the watermark ink pad.

13 Cut out the circular image and attach it to the inside of the card using double-sided tape, aligning it accurately with the aperture.

For the turquoise card below I first stamped and embossed the image on to white card using a rubber stamp from the Heritage Rubber Stamp Co., Celt3XLS13, and then coloured it in with a high quality felt-tip pen, highlighting certain areas. For the background I used the same background script rubber stamp as I used in the Golden Knotwork project on page 13 (Heritage Rubber Stamp Co., Celt6XLS1). I used a watermark ink pad for a subtle pattern. I then wrapped the background in gold and turquoise organza ribbon before attaching the central motif.

The tall, thin card on the right uses a stamped image of a labyrinth (Blade Rubber Stamps, 'Chartres') – a highly symbolic image often seen in Celtic and later Christian art. The background was stamped using a watermark ink pad, and the same design was stamped and embossed three times on to white card, cut out and glued on to the front of the card.

There is no reason why you cannot use pretty pastel colours with Celtic motifs. Below left I have stamped and embossed the image (Heritage Rubber Stamp Co., Celt4XLS5) on to white card and coloured it to match the colours of the card. I also added ribbon to give the card more texture.

Animal motifs are amongst the most popular Celtic images, and on the card shown below right I have combined a striking animal design (Heritage Rubber Stamp Co., Celt4XLS2) with red, gold and green to create a strong image that is perfect for Christmas.

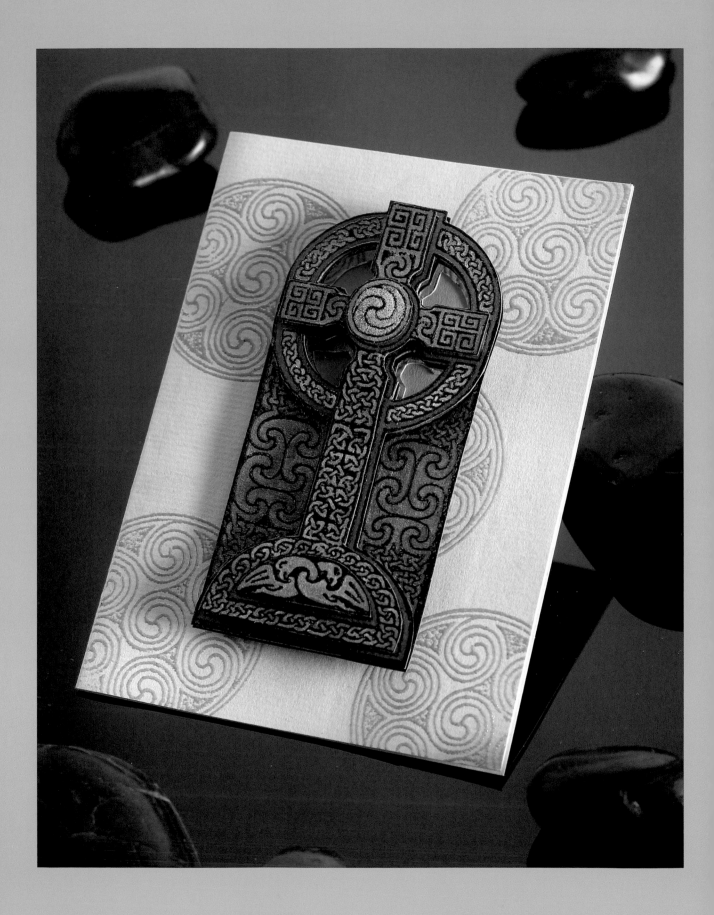

Emerald Cross

This project takes your stamping to another level: it involves layering several images to produce a three-dimensional (decoupaged) effect. Beautiful pearlescent watercolour paint, made from pigment powder and gum arabic, is used to colour the images, and a subtle patterned background created by heat embossing together with a tiny amount of silver glitter placed in the centre of the cross complete the card.

Tip

Some pigment powders already contain gum arabic. For these, just add one part water to two parts powder to create the watercolour paint.

1 To make the pearlescent watercolour paint, mix two parts pearlescent pigment powder with one part gum arabic using a spatula. Leave the mixture to dry overnight.

2 Stamp the Celtic cross design four times on the dark green card using the watermark ink pad.

YOU WILL NEED

Light green card blank, 10.5 x 14.5cm (4¼ x 5¾in)

Green pearlescent pigment powder

Gum arabic (fixative)

Spatula

Small plastic container with a lid

One sheet of A4 dark green card

Celtic cross rubber stamp, e.g. Heritage Rubber Stamp Co., Celt5XLS1

Circular Celtic spiral rubber stamp, e.g. Heritage Rubber Stamp Co., Celt3XLS4

Watermark ink pad

Dark green and light green embossing powders

Heat gun

Water brush

Craft knife

Cutting mat

Low-tack tape

Retractable pencil or sharp pencil

3D foam pads

PVA glue in a fine-tip applicator

Fine white glitter

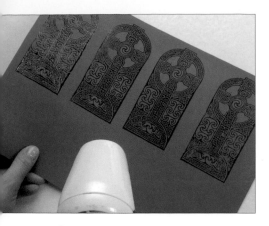

3 Cover the images with the dark green embossing powder, tip the excess back into the pot, and heat with a heat gun until the powder turns shiny.

4 Using a water brush and the green pearlescent paint, colour the panel on each side of the cross in one of the images.

5 Choose a second image, and colour the circle behind the cross.

6 In the third image, colour the cross itself, including the border around its base, and in the fourth colour the entwined birds and the circular spiral design in the centre.

7 Working on a cutting mat, use a craft knife to cut out the shapes between the cross and the circle in the first and second images. These will form the first two layers of the three-dimensional design.

8 From the third image, create the third layer by cutting out the cross and its base, and from the fourth (the top layer of the design) cut out the spiral that lies in the centre of the cross and the entwined birds within its base.

10 Emboss the design with light green embossing powder (see page 26). Position the bottom layer of the Celtic cross design accurately on the front of the card and attach it using low-tack tape. Outline the shapes within the top of the cross using a pencil.

9 Stamp the spiral design four or five times in a random pattern over the front of the card blank using the watermark ink pad.

11 Remove the Celtic cross, open out the card and place it on a cutting mat. Cut out the shapes marked on the card using a craft knife, cutting just outside the pencil lines.

12 Place 3D foam pads on the back of the first Celtic cross and attach it to the card, aligning the cut-out shapes.

13 Build up the layers in the order in which they were cut out. Secure each layer using 3D foam pads.

14 Apply PVA glue, using a fine-tip applicator, to the spiral design in the centre of the cross.

15 Sprinkle the spiral design with fine white glitter and tip off the excess to complete the card.

For this intricate cross I chose a blue theme and used good quality felt-tip pens to colour it in. I used an image from the Heritage Rubber Stamp Co., Celt2XLS2, and embossed it in silver twice. For the frame I used the stamp Celt5XLS3, also from the Heritage Rubber Stamp Co., and trimmed it to the inside edge.

For the blue, circular design I used watercolour paper as the base for the stamped and embossed image, for which I used a stamp from the Heritage Rubber Stamp Co., Celt4XLS4. This created texture on the embossed image, reminiscent of the movement of water. I also added some fine white glitter, as described in the project.

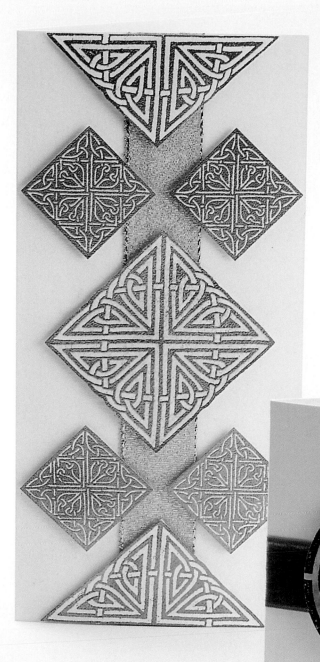

A monochromatic card is perfect for a wedding; just change the colour if gold is not your favourite. I use two stamps that have the same image but in different sizes – Heritage Rubber Stamp Co., Celt3XLS12 and CeltLS15. I use some gold ribbon on the back to add more texture. Once trimmed, the stamped images are attached with 3D foam pads for a three-dimensional effect.

For the card below I used the Heritage Rubber Stamp Co., Celt4XLS8 rubber stamp and purple embossing powder, then coloured in the image with felt-tip pens and finished it off with glitter. Velvet ribbon always has a very special feel about it and adds extra texture to the card.

Copper Script

Using thin metal sheets may be daunting at first, but it is actually a very easy and rewarding medium to work with. Here I have embossed a raised design on to the metal using a brass stencil, and coloured it using alcohol inks. These dry to a rich, jewel-like finish that works perfectly to create the ancient feel of this card.

YOU WILL NEED

One burgundy card blank, 12.5 x 16cm (5 x 6¼in)

Lightweight copper sheet, approximately 10cm (4in) square

One large sheet of scrap paper

One small piece of copper metallic paper, at least 12 x 15cm (4¾ x 6in)

Circular Celtic brass stencil, e.g. Dreamweaver, LL520

Large background script rubber stamp, e.g. Heritage Rubber Stamp Co., Celt6XLS1

Low-tack tape

Foam mat

Large and fine stump tools

Round-ended and pointed embossing tools

Black embossing paste

Palette knife

Piece of thin chipboard

Scissors

Alcohol inks in four different shades (reds, browns and oranges)

Alcohol ink applicator and blending solution

Cotton bud

Watermark ink pad

Heat gun

Dusty pink embossing powder

Adhesive roller

Large glue dots

1 Attach the circular brass stencil to the lightweight copper sheet using low-tack tape. Place it on a foam mat.

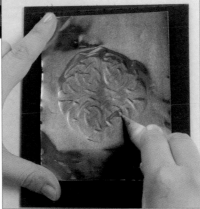

2 Turn the metal over and rub over the stencil with a large stump tool to reveal the design.

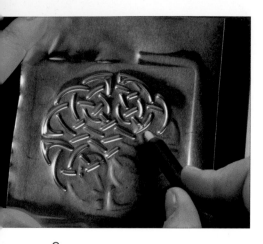

4 Repeat using a pointed embossing tool to accentuate the design further and bring out the fine detail.

3 Strengthen the design by going over the indentations with a round-ended embossing tool.

5 Finally, go over the indentations again with a fine stump tool to smooth them.

6 Turn the metal over and remove the stencil.

7 Turn the metal over again, and spread black embossing paste over the back of the design using a palette knife. The paste is forced into the indentations, which helps to hold them in place and prevents them from being flattened.

8 Cut a square piece of thin chipboard just slighly larger than the stencilled design. Attach the board to the back of the design using an adhesive roller, and trim off the corners of the metal sheet.

9 Fold the sides of the metal over the chipboard square, turn the design over so that it is face up, and flatten the edges and sharpen the corners using the large stump tool.

10 Place a drop of each of the four alcohol inks on the pad of the applicator so that they merge together.

11 Dab the ink firmly over the surface of the design.

12 Add more ink to the applicator and apply another layer of colour to create a mottled effect. Repeat this as many times as you wish, then leave to dry.

13 Use alcohol ink blending solution applied with a cotton bud to remove the ink from the raised parts of the design. If you accidentally remove ink from the background, simply apply more ink.

14 Cut a piece of copper metallic card so that it is 1cm (½in) smaller all round than the card blank. Apply the watermark ink pad to the background stamp, and stamp the image on to the copper paper.

15 Emboss the stamped image using dusty rose embossing powder.

16 Attach the stamped copper paper to the card blank using the adhesive roller, than attach the embossed metal design using large glue dots. Off-set it so that it is positioned slightly higher than the centre line and aligned with the right-hand edge of the copper paper.

For the tall card below right, use a black metal sheet and emboss it using a brass stencil (Marianne Design, CT6004), then apply alcohol inks on top. Trim the edges and use a tracing wheel or a piercing tool to add a border each side of the metal embossed image.

A cool look for copper, shown on the card below left, is to heat it, which causes the copper to change colour. The best way to do this is to emboss the copper first and then apply the heat with a hand-held heat gun – the type used by chefs is better for this than craft heat guns, as they produce more heat. Once the colour has changed and the metal has cooled down, apply embossing paste to the back and attach the metal to the card. Finish the card off with a crystal in the centre.

To make the card shown below left, use a silver metal sheet and emboss it using a brass stencil (Marianne Design, CT6007). To create the matt effect, use a metal brush and brush over the top of the metal with circular motions. Apply alcohol inks on top. Attach the motif to a piece of card stamped with a background image (here I have used Heritage Rubber Stamp Co., Celt6XLS2) and attach this to a card blank, overhanging one edge.

Try stamping on to metal using a solvent ink pad. On the card shown below I stamped on to silver metal sheet with white ink and let it dry for a couple of minutes. I then embossed the metal border using a mould, which I used in exactly the same way as a brass stencil. Finally I glued both the border and the central motif on to the card using strong adhesive.

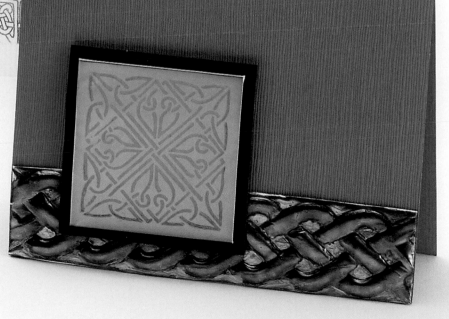

Spiral of Light

When it comes to adding impact to your cards, there is nothing as fun and as amazing as alcohol inks. These beautiful inks allow you to colour any non-porous surface, and will dry instantly. The inks blend together even when dry, allowing you continually to add different amounts of various colours until the desired effect is achieved. The addition of tiny patches of artificial gold leaf makes it glimmer and sparkle as it catches the light, enhancing the jewel-like quality of this card.

Template for the design, actual size. (Reproduced from Celtic Designs *by Courtney Davis)*

YOU WILL NEED

Dark green pearlescent card blank, 10.5cm (4¼in) square

One piece of black card, at least 9cm (3½in) square

One piece of gold metallic card, at least 9cm (3½in) square

One sheet of A4 transparency paper

One sheet of A4 photocopier paper

One sheet of scrap paper

Alcohol inks in various golds and greens

Alcohol ink applicator

Alcohol ink blending solution

Cotton bud

Pinpoint roller glue pen

Small pieces of imitation gold leaf

Adhesive roller

PVA glue in a fine-tip applicator

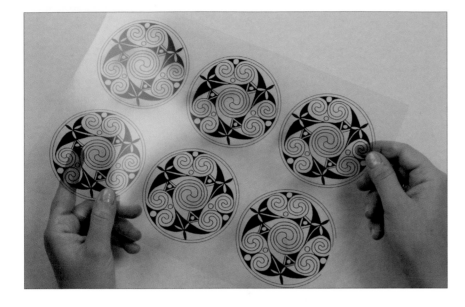

1 Make several copies of the design on an A4 sheet of transparency paper. Do this by first copying the design several times on to a sheet of white photocopier paper, and then copying this on to transparency paper.

2 Choose the best quality image, cut it out and place it face down on a piece of scrap paper. Place drops of alcohol ink in various shades of gold and green so that they blend together on the pad.

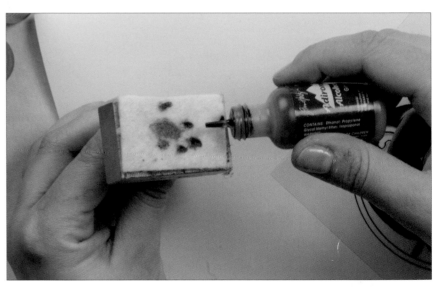

3 Stamp firmly over the back of the design. Build up several layers of colour, turning the design over regularly and varying the inks used to achieve the required effect.

4 Remove the ink from the tiny circles on the design using alcohol ink blending solution applied with a cotton bud.

5 Apply a thin coat of low-tack glue to each circle using a pinpoint roller glue pen.

6 Lay small pieces of imitation gold leaf over each circle.

8 Trim the black card so that it is approximately 1cm (½in) smaller all round than the card blank, and cut a piece of gold metallic card just slightly smaller than this. Mount the two pieces of card on the card blank using the adhesive roller.

7 Turn the design face up and trim carefully around the outside using a sharp pair of scissors. Retain the outer black line.

9 Attach the design to the front of the card using PVA glue applied to the dark areas of the design only.

To create the intricate pattern on the card below is really easy. Make two copies of your chosen design on acetate and then apply alcohol inks to both of them. Remove the inks from the circles. Once dried, trim the designs to size and attach them on top of glitter paper so that it shows through the gaps.

For the card on the right, I matched the colours of the patterned paper with the alcohol inks, and applied transparent glitter glue to highlight the pattern on the main motif. After the glitter glue had dried (it takes a while for glitter glue to dry on acetate), I trimmed around the motif and attached it to the card.

The design below left is very similar to the project; the difference is that the clear gaps are left clear so that the texture of the card underneath shows through. Finish the card by stamping an image in each corner using gold ink.

For a card with a difference, position the main motif over the top edge of the card, as on the design shown below right. Just make sure there is an envelope large enough for the entire card! Stamp the frame (Heritage Rubber Stamp Co., Celt4XLS3) on to turquoise card and trim around it, glue a piece of silver paper on the back and then attach the complete motif to the card. Apply alcohol inks to the peacock and attach it to the inside of the frame.

Index